P9-AGC-513

CORPORATE DIRECTOR'S GUIDEBOOK

SECOND EDITION

COMMITTEE ON CORPORATE LAWS
SECTION OF BUSINESS LAW

AMERICAN BAR ASSOCIATION

Cover design by Emily Friel.

The materials contained herein represent the opinions of the authors and editors and should not be construed to be the action of either the American Bar Association or the Section of Business Law unless adopted pursuant to the bylaws of the Association.

Nothing contained in this book is to be considered as the rendering of legal advice for specific cases, and readers are responsible for obtaining such advice from their own legal counsel. This book and any forms and agreements herein are intended for educational and informational purposes only.

© 1994 American Bar Association. All rights reserved.
Printed in the United States of America.

Library of Congress Catalog Card Number 94-70987
ISBN 0-89707-994-9

Discounts are available for books ordered in bulk. Special consideration is given to state bars, CLE programs, and other bar-related organizations. Inquire at Publications Planning & Marketing, American Bar Association, 750 North Lake Shore Drive, Chicago, Illinois 60611.

99 98 97   8 7 6

COMMITTEE ON CORPORATE LAWS

(1991   1994)

Jean Allard
Chicago, Illinois

John Page Austin
San Francisco, California

Thomas E. Baker
Houston, Texas

R. Franklin Balotti
Wilmington, Delaware

Dennis J. Block
New York, New York

Stephen W. Carr
Boston, Massachusetts

Henry E. Chatham
Jackson, Mississippi

James H. Cheek
Nashville, Tennessee

Nicolas E. Chimicles
Haverford, Pennsylvania

Albert W. Driver
New York, New York

Melvin A. Eisenberg
Berkeley, California

Victor Futter
New York, New York

Janet T. Geldzahler
New York, New York

Jean W. Gleason
Washington, D.C.

Elliot Goldstein
Atlanta, Georgia

Charles Hansen
St. Louis, Missouri

Joseph Hinsey, IV
Boston, Massachusetts

Arne Hovdesven
New York, New York

Michael L. Jamieson
Tampa, Florida

Stephen J. Leacock
Chicago, Illinois

Simon M. Lorne
Washington, D.C.

James I. Lotstein
Hartford, Connecticut

Morey W. McDaniel
Danbury, Connecticut

Karen W. McDonie
Philadelphia, Pennsylvania

James P. Melican
Purchase, New York

A. Gilchrist Sparks, III
Wilmington, Delaware

Frank R. Morris, Jr.
Columbus, Ohio

William H. Steinbrink
Cleveland, Ohio

David E. Nelson
San Francisco, California

John T. Subak
Philadelphia, Pennsylvania

Sidney J. Nurkin
Atlanta, Georgia

Robert W. Trafford
Columbus, Ohio

Honorable William T. Quillen
Wilmington, Delaware

James F. Tune
Seattle, Washington

Donald A. Scott
Philadelphia, Pennsylvania

Honorable E. Norman Veasey
Wilmington, Delaware

Mary Siegel
Washington, D.C.

Robert M. Walmsley, Jr.
New Orleans, Louisiana

Robert W. Smith
Baltimore, Maryland

James B. Zimpritch
Portland, Maine

A. A. Sommer, Jr.
Washington, D.C.

CONTENTS

v

INTRODUCTION

Why revise the extremely successful 1978 version of the ABA Section of Business Law's *Corporate Director's Guidebook*? It has been a much praised and popular publication. In addition to the many readers of *The Business Lawyer*, in which the final version of the Guidebook was published in April of 1978, more than 20,000 reprints have been sold to lawyers, corporate directors, business executives, academics, and other interested readers. Further, the legal analysis on which it is based has been broadly supported and frequently cited. So, why tinker with success?

The major and most compelling reasons are tied closely to evolution and growth. The fifteen years that have passed since publication of the Guidebook have witnessed a significant increase in the number of relevant precedents and studies of the subject. In summary, a lot has happened, and continues to happen, in the corporate governance world since 1978, including:

- Tremendous pressure initiated during the "takeover years," particularly in the courts of Delaware, to determine the proper implementation of previously abstract principles.
- Increased interest by large institutional investors in corporate governance, particularly the structure, composition, and role of the board of directors; takeover defense strategies; and executive compensation matters.
- Increased activism of directors in implementing the board's monitoring responsibilities—to the extent of forcing top management reorganizations.
- Publication of drafts of the American Law Institute's (ALI) *Principles of Corporate Governance*, which brought significant clarifications of corporate law and also generated controversy and competing analytical efforts.

1

- Increased use of board committees, bringing directors into closer working relationships with each other, members of management, and consultants.
- Greater Securities and Exchange Commission (SEC) interest in what might be called "corporate governance through disclosure"—for example, revised proxy rules relating to shareholder proposals and executive compensation.

We also decided to review issues treated in a series of reports and articles published in *The Business Lawyer*, particularly the 1979 report of the Committee on Corporate Laws on *The Overview Committees of the Board of Directors*.

Having expanded here, reduced there, and relocated throughout, we also have made some structural changes in the Guidebook. We have deleted the "proposed model" of the board of a publicly held corporation for two reasons: first, much of this material is now found in the discussion of the structure of the board and its committees; and second, developments in applicable law have removed much of the need for the tentativeness reflected in the concept of a model. In the interest of "user friendliness," we have avoided the use of footnotes and instead have included a bibliography.

As in 1978, the Model Business Corporation Act (Model Act), which itself has been extensively revised during this period, is the primary statutory frame of reference for this Guidebook. We also have included elements drawn from the ALI Corporate Governance Project and reports of The Business Roundtable. Our principal frame of reference and source of material has been the 1978 Guidebook, an outstanding job under any circumstances and, considering the accuracy of its predictions, a remarkable achievement.

- reviewing the process of providing appropriate financial and operational information to decisionmakers (including board members); and
- evaluating the overall effectiveness of the board.

Stated broadly, the principal responsibility of a corporate director is to promote the best interests of the corporation and its shareholders in directing the corporation's business and affairs.

In so doing, the director should give primary consideration to long-term economic objectives. However, a director should also be concerned that the corporation conducts its affairs with due appreciation of public expectations, taking into consideration trends in the law and ethical standards. Furthermore, pursuit of the corporation's economic objectives may include consideration of the effect of corporate policies and operations upon the corporation's employees, the public, and the environment. Many states have adopted legislation expressly recognizing that corporate directors may consider the effect of corporate action on constituencies other than shareholders, such as employees, local communities, suppliers, and customers. Nevertheless, the law normally does not hold a corporate director directly responsible to constituencies other than shareholders in the formulation of corporate policy.

A director should exercise independent judgment for the overall benefit of the corporation and all of its shareholders, even if elected at the request of a controlling shareholder, a union, a creditor, or an institutional shareholder or pursuant to contractual rights.

To be effective, a director should become familiar with the corporation's business. This knowledge should enable the director to make an independent evaluation of senior management performance and allow the director to join with other directors to support, challenge, and reward management as warranted. Accordingly, all directors should have a basic understanding of the:

- principal operational and financial objectives, strategies, and plans of the corporation;
- results of operations and financial condition of the corporation and of any significant subsidiaries and business segments; and

- relative standing of the business segments within the corporation and vis-a-vis competitors.

In addition, a director should be satisfied that an effective system is in place for periodic and timely reporting to the board on the following matters:

- current business and financial performance, the degree of achievement of approved objectives, and the need to address forward-planning issues;
- financial statements, with appropriate segment or divisional breakdowns;
- compliance with law and corporate policies; and
- material litigation and regulatory matters.

Finally, directors should do their homework. They should review board and committee meeting agendas and related materials sufficiently in advance of meetings to enable them to participate in an informed manner. They should receive and review reports of all board and committee meetings.

B. Areas of Special Concern

A director should be particularly concerned that the corporation has established and implemented programs designed to meet the following inquiries.

1. Quality of Disclosure. Do the corporation's disclosure documents, such as annual and quarterly reports to shareholders, proxy statements, and prospectuses, fairly present all material information? A director's primary responsibility in the disclosure process is to be satisfied that procedures are being followed that are likely to result in accurate and appropriate corporate disclosure. Although management has the primary responsibility for implementing these processes, directors should review drafts of the annual reports, proxy statements, and prospectuses.

2. Compliance with Law. Does the corporation have appropriate policies directed to compliance with applicable laws and regulations? For example, when appropriate, does the board receive periodic reports regarding compliance with environmental laws, including estimates of the costs of environmental compliance?

Employees should be informed of corporate policies directed to compliance with applicable laws, including personnel policies designed to comply with health and safety, antidiscrimination and employment laws, and the securities laws, particularly those prohibiting insider trading. The corporation should establish appropriate procedures for monitoring compliance. All persons involved in the compliance process should have direct access to the general counsel or a designee so that sensitive compliance matters may be raised for consideration.

3. **Approval of Commitments.** Is there a functioning and effective system in place for approval of commitments of the corporation's financial and commercial resources? Although board approval of all or even most of these commitments is not necessary, the board should be satisfied that such a system exists.

4. **Adequacy of Internal Controls.** Does the corporation maintain adequate systems of internal controls?

5. **Protection of Assets.** Does the board receive periodic reports describing the corporation's program for the protection of its assets? In addition to insurance arrangements, such a program should include procedures for protecting intellectual property and safeguarding confidential corporate information.

6. **Counseling of Directors.** Does the corporation provide board members competent legal advice regarding the corporation's affairs and the conduct of its directors? A director should be able to communicate directly with the corporation's principal external and internal advisers, including its auditors, legal counsel, and, when such relationships exist, its investment banking and executive compensation advisers. Further, there may be occasions when an outside adviser should be specially retained to assist the board or a committee in connection with a particular matter.

C. Disagreement

If, after a thorough discussion, a director disagrees with any significant action to be taken by the board, the director may vote against the proposal and request that the dissent be recorded in the meeting's minutes. Except in unusual circumstances, taking such a position should not cause a director to consider resigning. However, if a director believes that information being disclosed by the corporation is inadequate, incomplete, or incorrect or that management is not dealing with the directors, the shareholders, or the public in good faith, the director should see that corrective action is taken, replace management, or resign.

SECTION 3

Legal Analysis of the Basic Duties of a Director

The legal obligations of directors fall into two broad categories: a duty of care and a duty of loyalty.

Model Act Section 8.30 provides that a director shall discharge the director's duties, including duties as a member of a committee (i) in good faith, (ii) with the care an ordinarily prudent person in a like position would exercise under similar circumstances, and (iii) in a manner he or she reasonably believes to be in the best interests of the corporation.

A. The Duty of Care

Parsing Section 8.30 is helpful in analyzing the components of a director's duties:

- *in good faith*—acting honestly; not to act, or cause the corporation to act, in an unlawful way; purporting to rely upon information that a director knows to be untrue will not be considered acting in good faith;
- *care*—expressing the need to pay attention and to act diligently and reasonably;
- *ordinarily prudent person*—incorporating the basic attributes of common sense, practical wisdom, and informed judgment;
- *in a like position*—recognizing that the nature and extent of the corporate director's role will vary depending upon

such factors as the background and qualifications of the director, and the size, complexity, and location of the enterprise's activities;

■ *under similar circumstances*—recognizing that the nature and extent of the oversight will vary, depending upon the corporation concerned and the factual situation presented;

■ *reasonably believes*—establishing that the standard of conduct is objective, not subjective; and

■ *best interests of the corporation*—emphasizing the corporate director's primary allegiance to the corporation.

B. Aspects of the Duty of Care

Compliance with the duty of care is based on diligence applied to the ordinary and extraordinary needs of the corporation, including the following:

1. Regular Attendance. Directors are expected to attend and participate, either in person or by telephone (to the extent authorized by law), in board and committee meetings. Generally, directors cannot vote or participate by proxy; a director's personal participation is required.

2. Agendas. While agendas for both board and committee meetings are generally initiated by management, a director is entitled to place matters the director reasonably considers to be important on the agenda.

3. Adequate Information. Management should supply directors with sufficient information to keep them properly informed about the business and affairs of the corporation. When specific actions are contemplated, directors should receive appropriate information sufficiently in advance of the board or committee meeting to allow study of and reflection on the issues raised. Important time-sensitive materials that become available between meetings should be distributed to board members. On their part, directors are expected to review the materials supplied. If sufficient information is not made available in a timely manner, the director should request that action be delayed until the desired information is made available and studied. If a director believes the board is not regularly provided with enough information to enable the director to vote or act in an informed manner, and is unsuccessful in efforts to remedy the situation, the director should consider changing management or resigning.

4. **The Right to Rely on Others and the Need to Keep Informed.** A director is entitled to rely on reports, opinions, information, and statements (including financial statements and other financial data) presented by (i) the corporation's officers or employees whom the director reasonably believes to be reliable and competent in the matters presented, (ii) legal counsel, public accountants, or other persons as to matters that the director reasonably believes to be within their professional or expert competence, and (iii) duly authorized committees of the board on which the director does not serve, unless in any such cases the director has knowledge that would make such reliance unwarranted. However, a director relying on others has a responsibility to keep informed of the efforts of those to whom the work has been delegated. The extent of this review function will vary depending upon the nature and importance of the matter in question.

5. **Inquiry.** A director should make inquiry when alerted by the circumstances.

C. The Business Judgment Rule

The duty of care is qualified by the business judgment rule. This rule, well established in case law, protects a disinterested director from personal liability to the corporation and its shareholders, even though a corporate decision the director has approved turns out to be unwise or unsuccessful. In reviewing a disinterested director's conduct, a court will not substitute its judgment (particularly in hindsight) for that of the director, provided the director:

- acted in good faith;
- was reasonably informed; and
- rationally believed the action taken was in the best interests of the corporation.

Accordingly, the business judgment rule, unlike the standards of conduct encompassed in the duties of care and loyalty, is not a description of a duty or standard used to determine whether a breach of duty has occurred; rather it is an element of judicial review used in analyzing director conduct to determine whether a director should be held personally liable. If the rule applies, directors are presumed to have exercised their judgment in good faith and in the rational belief that the actions were taken in the best interests of the corporation. In such circumstances, a court will not examine the merits of a decision of directors or substitute its judgment regarding the wisdom of a decision within the business judgment of directors.

D. The Duty of Loyalty

The duty of loyalty requires directors to exercise their powers in the interests of the corporation and not in the directors' own interest or in the interest of another person (including a family member) or organization. Simply put, directors should not use their corporate position to make a personal profit or gain or for other personal advantage. In themselves, conflicts of interest are not inherently improper. It is the manner in which an interested director and the board deal with a conflict that determines the propriety of the transaction and of the director's conduct. The duty of loyalty has a number of specific applications.

1. **Conflicts of Interest.** Directors should be alert and sensitive to any interest they may have that might be considered to conflict with the best interests of the corporation. When a director, directly or indirectly, has a financial or personal interest in a contract or transaction to which the corporation is to be a party, or is contemplating entering into a transaction that involves use of corporate assets or competition against the corporation, the director is considered to be "interested" in the matter. An interested director should seek approval by disinterested directors of interested transactions or conduct and should disclose that interest and describe to the board members all material facts concerning the matter known to the director. The board members should then act on the matter with complete candor, accuracy, and inclusiveness before the action is taken. An interested director

should abstain from voting on the matter and, in most situations, leave the meeting while the disinterested directors discuss and vote.

A corporation often will enter into transactions with other corporations that share a common director. When possible, the common directors, after having disclosed all pertinent information known to them, should avoid personal participation in approving the transaction and leave review and action to disinterested directors. State statutes usually include procedures that may be used to authorize or ratify transactions with interested directors and should be followed.

2. Corporate Opportunity. In some circumstances the duty of loyalty requires that a director make a business opportunity available to the corporation before the director may pursue the opportunity for the director's own or another's account. Whether such an opportunity must first be offered to the corporation will often depend on one or more of the following factors:

- The circumstances in which the director became aware of the opportunity;
- The significance of the opportunity to the corporation and the degree of interest of the corporation in the opportunity;
- Whether the opportunity relates to the corporation's existing or contemplated business; and
- Whether there is a reasonable basis for the corporation to expect that the director should make the opportunity available to the corporation.

If a director believes that a contemplated transaction might be found to be a corporate opportunity, the director should make full disclosure to the board and seek its authorization to pursue the opportunity.

E. Confidentiality
A director should deal in confidence with all matters involving the corporation until such time as there has been general public disclosure. A director of a publicly held corporation is often asked by investors and investment advisers to comment on

sensitive issues, particularly financial information; however, an individual director is not usually authorized to be a spokesperson for the corporation and, particularly when market-sensitive information is involved, should avoid responding to such inquiries. A director normally should refer investors, market professionals, and the media to the chief executive officer (CEO) or other individual designated by the corporation.

F. Fairness, Documentation, and Policies

1. Fairness to the Corporation. Disinterested directors reviewing the fairness of a transaction having self-dealing elements are essentially seeking to determine whether the proposed transaction is on at least as favorable terms to the corporation as might be available from other persons or entities, whether it is reasonably likely to further the corporation's business activities, and whether the process by which the decision is approved or ratified is fair. If minority shareholders could be adversely affected, the directors should be especially concerned that the minority receives fair treatment. This concern is heightened when a dominant shareholder or shareholder group has a divergent or conflicting interest.

2. Documentation of Conflicts. As a general rule, disclosures of conflicts of interest and the results of the directors' consideration of the matter should be documented in the minutes or reports of the meeting.

3. Written Policies. Many corporations have adopted written policies on conflicts of interest (often in conjunction with other major policies, such as trading in the corporation's securities and compliance with antitrust, environmental, and antidiscrimination laws) and procedures to monitor compliance with these policies.

Board Structure
and Operations

Boards of directors should be structured and their proceedings conducted in a way calculated to encourage, reinforce, and demonstrate the board's role as an independent and informed monitor of the conduct of the corporation's affairs and the performance of its management. Board structure and practice will, over time, significantly affect the extent to which a board of directors is likely to exercise its powers and discharge its obligations in a manner that effectively advances corporate objectives.

No single governance structure fits all publicly held corporations, and there is considerable diversity of organizational styles. Each corporation should develop a governance structure that is appropriate to its nature and circumstances.

A. Board Composition

In determining board composition, the focus should be on the personal qualities and business experience of the individual directors, and the overall mix of experience, independence, and diversity of backgrounds likely to make the board of directors, as a body, most effective in monitoring the performance of the corporation.

If the board of directors is to function effectively, it must exercise independent judgment in carrying out its responsibilities. It is also important that the board not only exercise independent judgment, but also be perceived by shareholders and other corporate constituencies to be doing so. To encourage an environment likely to nurture independence in fact and to communicate that appearance of independence, at least a majority of members of the boards of publicly held corporations should be independent of management.

A director who is an executive officer of the corporation or who is an employee devoting substantially full time and attention to the affairs of the corporation, one of its subsidiaries, or any other corporation controlling or controlled by the corporation, will be viewed as a management director. A director who has not been active in the management of the corporation and who is therefore otherwise properly described as a nonmanagement director may nonetheless have some relationship with the corporation or its management that could be viewed as interfering with the exercise of independent judgment. As a general rule a director will be viewed as independent only if he or she is a nonmanagement director free of any material business or professional relationship with the corporation or its management. The circumstances and various relationships that have been often identified as presumptively inconsistent with independence include:

- a close family or similar relationship with a member of key management;
- any business or professional relationship with the corporation that is material to the corporation or the director; and
- any ongoing business or professional relationship with the corporation, whether or not material in an economic sense, that involves continued dealings with management, such as the relationship between a corporation and investment bankers or corporate counsel.

B. Board Leadership

There is considerable discussion of different ways to strengthen the role of independent directors. Suggestions include having:

- an independent director serve as chair of the board, thus separating the roles of chair and CEO;

- the independent directors designate one of the members to act as a lead director, if the CEO serves also as chair;
- members of board oversight committees, a majority of whom should be independent, choose their own committee chairs rather than having the chairs designated by the CEO;
- the independent directors meet periodically as a body to review the performance of management and of the members of the board; and
- independent directors available to meet with substantial shareholders, particularly when those shareholders are not satisfied with responses they have received from management.

Some of these suggestions are controversial. Although few have yet been widely implemented or represent common practice, many boards of large, publicly held corporations will likely be addressing these issues in the coming years.

C. Size of Board of Directors

Each corporation should determine the best board size to accommodate key objectives, including:

- sufficient independent directors to perform the functions normally assigned to the oversight committees; and
- effective functioning in terms of discussion and decision making.

Other factors that might influence board size are the special needs of certain types of corporations to maintain a strong community presence, to establish or maintain relationships with customers or other constituencies, and to respond to other factors that may be idiosyncratic to the corporation or industry in which it operates. In accommodating these other needs, the board size should not be expanded to such an extent as to interfere with its effective functioning.

There is substantial variation in the size of boards of publicly owned corporations. Banks, insurance companies, and larger corporations with complex businesses typically have larger boards, averaging about fifteen members. By contrast, the boards of smaller industrial corporations now average about eight or nine members. This may reflect the emerging consensus that, except perhaps in the very largest and most complex corporations, smaller boards (those with twelve or fewer members) function more effectively than larger boards. Directors serving on a smaller board have more opportunity to ask questions, exchange opinions, and otherwise participate in board deliberations. Larger boards may make effective participation by individual members more difficult. Large boards often resolve this problem through delegation of significant activities to various board committees.

D. Director's Time Commitment

Nonmanagement directors are expected to devote substantial time and attention to the affairs of the corporation—at least sufficient time to permit the directors to prepare for and attend meetings of the board and board committees and to keep themselves informed about the corporation's business.

The time required varies widely. Surveys indicate that, on the average, directors of public companies devote about 100 hours to board service each year—approximately the time required for six full days of meetings and six full days of preparation for meetings and reviewing other materials. The time commitment expected of directors is a subject that should be reviewed by the board and communicated to existing and prospective directors. Directors should take care not to overcommit themselves, and nominating committees should consider a board candidate's ability to devote the necessary time. In times of crises or in similar circumstances, directors of public companies will be required to devote a substantial amount of time in addition to their normal commitment to the corporation.

E. Board Compensation

Directors have an unavoidable conflict of interest in fixing their own compensation. That conflict is not reduced if the recommendation is made by management. When directors recognize they have the responsibility to determine their own compensation, they are more likely to make sure they have the data necessary to reach a fair conclusion. That includes data on comparable companies, together with analysis of any special factors that may relate to the particular corporation.

Directors should be fairly compensated. A major objective of board compensation plans should be to compensate directors fairly and in doing so to align their financial interests with the long-range objectives of the shareholders. Directors' compensation may take a number of different forms, including annual retainers and attendance fees for board and committee meetings, deferred compensation plans, retirement programs, matching educational or charitable contributions, and accident or other insurance.

The board should be alert to avoid compensation policies or the use of corporate perquisites that might tend to subvert the independence of its outside directors or divert their focus from proper long-range corporate objectives. In this respect, some believe that stock options and restricted stock grants to directors strengthen directors' interest in the overall success of the corporation, while others believe that these forms of compensation tend to align directors' interests too closely with those of management.

F. Quality of Information

The quality of information made available to directors will significantly affect their ability to perform their roles effectively. Information submitted to the directors should be relevant, concise and timely, well organized, supported by any background or historical data necessary or useful to place the information in context, and designed to inform directors of material aspects of the corporation's business, performance, and prospects. Information should be provided sufficiently in advance to provide time for thoughtful reflection and meaningful participation by the directors.

G. Meetings

The number of board meetings a corporation finds necessary or useful varies with the circumstances. Some boards prefer more frequent and shorter meetings. Others prefer fewer but lengthier meetings. On average, boards of directors of publicly owned corporations meet six times a year.

Time at board and committee meetings should be budgeted carefully. A balance should be sought between management presentations and discussion among directors and management. Written reports that can be given concisely and effectively in advance should be furnished.

There are special occasions when the nonmanagement directors may wish to meet alone for consideration of a takeover, leveraged buyout, or similar situation. In such cases special advisers, including legal counsel, may be asked to help the directors address the issues at hand. Whether the meeting is structured as a special committee meeting or as part of a regular board meeting, holding such a meeting is an appropriate exercise of directors' rights.

H. Control of the Agenda

The question of what will be discussed and acted on by the board is typically initially determined by management. Directors should be given an opportunity to place items on the agenda. Further, the board should satisfy itself that there is an overall annual agenda of matters that require recurring and focused attention, such as achievement of principal operational or financial objectives and review of the performance of the CEO and other members of executive management.

SECTION 5

Rights of Directors

The law recognizes certain prerogatives as necessary to performance of a director's duties. Among the most important are the rights to:

- communicate with key executives, subject to reasonable time constraints;
- inspect books and records and, subject to a director's duty not to disclose the corporation's confidential information, to be provided with copies of such data as the director may reasonably request;
- inspect plants and facilities as reasonably required for the performance of duties;
- be given notice of all meetings in which the director is entitled to participate;
- receive copies of all board and committee meeting minutes or reports (subject to a director's duty not to disclose the corporation's confidential information), whether or not the director is a member of the committee; and
- communicate directly with the corporation's principal external and internal advisers and, when appropriate, obtain the advice, at the corporation's expense, of outside legal counsel, investment bankers, accountants, and other consultants.

Orientation of the
New Director

An individual considering an invitation to join a board should study both the corporation and the board and should accept a directorship only if confident of the competence and integrity of the top management and the other directors of the corporation. An individual asked to be a director should:

- meet with the CEO and possibly with other directors to discuss the principal issues facing the corporation and to determine the attitude of the CEO toward board activity, principally whether independent judgment is truly desired;
- review the corporation's recent principal public documents, such as the latest Form 10-K annual and 10-Q quarterly reports filed with the SEC, recent annual reports to shareholders, the most recent proxy statement, the corporation's latest prospectus, if one exists, and interim reports sent to shareholders since the end of the last fiscal year;
- become familiar with the roles of the corporation's inside and outside auditors and counsel;
- review examples of the internal financial statements used by management and the board, and examine relevant long-range forecasts, long-range plans, and consulting or similar studies produced during the past year or cur-

rently being used by the corporation as fundamental planning documents; and

■ review summaries of the corporation's directors and officers liability insurance and material litigation.

SECTION 7

Committees of the Board

Much of the work of the typical board of directors is performed in committee. This is recognized by regulatory bodies, institutional investors, and others urging more effective corporate governance. For example, the New York Stock Exchange (NYSE) requires listed companies to have an Audit Committee composed of independent directors, and the SEC proxy rules mandate reports from the Compensation Committee (if one exists) and strongly discourage interlocking and management directors on Compensation Committees. Similarly, key board committees with membership limited to independent directors are at the core of many proposals for effective corporate governance.

Diversity in board structure and size does not allow uniform mandates for a particular committee organization. A seven-member board necessarily divides its work differently than one with twenty directors. Some boards function almost entirely at the full board level; in other corporations the board usually acts upon legally required matters, and essentially all the work is handled by its committees, with their activities reported to and, in some cases, approved by the full board.

Practice also varies greatly in allocating responsibilities among particular committees. Recommendation of outside auditors and review of financial statements are almost always assigned to the Audit Committee. Review of legal compliance matters, on the other hand, may be handled by an Audit Committee, a Legal Compliance Committee, a Public Responsibility

Committee, or the full board. Any recommendations in this Guidebook that certain matters be considered by a particular committee are not meant to suggest a particular board structure or any specific division of committee responsibilities. The important point is that the matter be considered by some group of directors and, in appropriate instances, by directors who are independent of management and disinterested in the matter at hand.

Corporate law generally and Model Act Section 8.30 specifically permit a director to rely upon a committee on which the board member does not serve. The following basic procedures should be observed to justify reliance on committee action:

- The composition of the committee should be appropriate to its purpose. This includes relevant experience and independence from management by all or at least a majority of the members of such key committees as audit, nominating, and compensation.
- The full board should satisfy itself that its committees are following an appropriate schedule of meetings and have agendas and procedures to enable them to fulfill their delegated functions. Furthermore, the full board should be kept informed of committee activities. This includes periodic reports at board meetings and circulation of committee minutes and reports of meetings to all directors. As stated in Model Act Section 8.25(f), board members do not fulfill their responsibilities simply by delegating authority to a committee. The full board, including directors not on a particular committee, must make reasonable efforts to keep abreast of the activities of its committees.
- Actions taken by committees must observe the limits imposed by law. Model Act Section 8.25(e) and the corporate laws of most states limit the authority of committees with respect to certain board actions. For example, normally a committee may not declare dividends, fill board vacancies, amend bylaws or articles of incorporation, or authorize issuance of stock.
- The duties of each committee should be clearly defined, typically in bylaws or board resolutions. There should be a periodic review to ensure that the duties assigned are

both realistic and consistent with what the committee is actually doing.

■ From time to time committees undertake special duties and responsibilities. Usually, board or committee minutes or some other writing describing these duties and responsibilities assigned to or undertaken by a committee should be prepared and included in the corporation's records.

This Guidebook focuses only on board oversight committees and does not address such committees as executive, finance, and strategic planning. Each corporation needs to tailor the functions of these committees to its own needs. In doing so, particular care should be taken that their membership reflects the makeup of the full board. Thus, an Executive Committee that frequently acts on important matters (as opposed to being a standby resource acting only in emergency or administrative situations) should reflect the composition of the full board. It should not be composed solely of management directors. Furthermore, the Executive Committee should not be so powerful that the board is seen as having first- and second-class citizens.

If a director or officer is alleged to have engaged in conduct damaging to the corporation or violating some law, the corporate response and the extent to which the individual should be supported, terminated, or otherwise sanctioned should be based on reviews by officers and directors who have no interest in the matter. This may be handled by a committee specifically appointed for the purpose or by an appropriately organized existing committee.

There are special situations—tender offers, alleged misconduct by a director or officer, major criminal investigations, management buyouts—that may require special committee handling. These unique, sometimes life-threatening events are not treated here; neither are the difficult issues faced by special litigation committees appointed when derivative litigation is brought against directors.

SECTION 8

The Audit Committee

Since first recommended by the NYSE in 1939, the Audit Committee has become a common component of the corporate governance structure of public companies. It typically functions as an overseer of the corporation's financial reporting process and internal controls. The NYSE, the American Stock Exchange (ASE), and the NASDAQ National Market System (NASDAQ NMS) all require listed companies to establish and maintain Audit Committees consisting exclusively (in the case of the NYSE) or primarily (in the case of the ASE and the NASDAQ NMS) of independent directors.

A. Membership

Audit Committees typically consist of three to five independent directors. As with most committees, Audit Committees with relatively few members can act more efficiently. On the other hand, an Audit Committee with too few members may lack the diversity of experience necessary to be effective. To the extent practicable, members of Audit Committees should have a sufficient understanding of financial reporting and internal control principles to understand and help deal with material financial reporting and internal control issues. The most important qualifications, however, remain common sense, general intelligence, and an independent cast of mind.

The Audit Committee should be composed solely of independent directors. The NYSE requires that the members of the Audit Committee of a listed company be "independent of man-

27

agement and free from any relationship that, in the opinion of its board of directors, would interfere with the exercise of independent judgment as a committee member." The ASE and the NASDAQ NMS require that at least a majority of the members of an Audit Committee be similarly independent directors. Directors who are employed by the corporation do not qualify as independent directors. In addition, directors who are engaged in material business transactions with the corporation and directors who serve on a regular basis as professional advisers, legal counsel, or consultants for the corporation would normally not qualify as independent.

An Audit Committee generally will rely on a corporation's existing staff and its outside auditors for help in performing its duties and responsibilities. The committee should have direct access to financial, legal, and other staff and advisers of the corporation. Such advisers may assist the committee members in defining their roles and responsibilities, consult with committee members regarding a specific audit or other issues that may arise in the course of the committee's duties, and conduct independent investigations, studies, or tests. The committee should also have the authority to employ accountants, attorneys, or other advisers to assist the committee, though this power is typically used only in special circumstances.

B. Principal Functions

The principal functions of an Audit Committee will vary depending upon many factors, including the type, complexity, and size of the business involved; the sophistication of the corporation's internal controls; and the existence of past material errors, omissions, defalcations, or crimes.

The following list of recommended duties of Audit Committees is drawn in substantial part from the ALI's *Principles of Corporate Governance*:

- Recommend which firm to engage as the corporation's external auditor and whether to terminate that relationship.
- Review the external auditor's compensation, the proposed terms of its engagement, and its independence.

- Review the appointment and replacement of the senior internal auditing executive, if any.
- Serve as a channel of communication between the external auditor and the board and between the senior internal auditing executive, if any, and the board.
- Review the results of each external audit, including any qualifications in the external auditor's opinion, any related management letter, management's responses to recommendations made by the external auditor in connection with the audit, reports submitted to the Audit Committee by the internal auditing department that are material to the corporation as a whole, and management's responses to those reports.
- Review the corporation's annual financial statements and any significant disputes between management and the external auditor that arose in connection with the preparation of those financial statements.
- Consider, in consultation with the external auditor and the senior internal auditing executive, if any, the adequacy of the corporation's internal financial controls. Among other things, these controls must be designed to provide reasonable assurance that the corporation's publicly reported financial statements are presented fairly in conformity with generally accepted accounting principles.
- Consider major changes and other major questions of choice regarding the appropriate auditing and accounting principles and practices to be followed when preparing the corporation's financial statements.
- Review the procedures employed by the corporation in preparing published financial statements and related management commentaries.
- Meet periodically with management to review the corporation's major financial risk exposures.

C. Independent Audit
The Audit Committee should meet with the corporation's external auditor during the planning of the audit to review the planning and staffing of the audit and to discuss any particular areas that may require emphasis or special procedures during

that year's audit. After the completion of the corporation's annual audit, the Audit Committee should review with the external auditor any problems or difficulties that the external auditor may have encountered, any management letter provided by the accountants, and the corporation's response to that letter. With respect to any areas identified as requiring special audit procedures, the Audit Committee should review the findings of the independent auditor and determine whether revisions to corporate policy or procedures are necessary. The Audit Committee should periodically evaluate the degree of independence of the corporation's external auditor, including any effect of nonaudit services provided by the auditors.

D. Internal Audit

Most large public companies have an internal audit department. If an internal audit department exists, the Audit Committee should routinely meet with the senior internal auditing executive to discuss special problems or issues that may have been encountered by the internal auditors and review the implementation of any recommended corrective actions.

E. Meetings with Auditors

Most meetings with external and internal auditors will be conducted in the presence of the chief financial officer and other members of management responsible for financial affairs. In addition, the Audit Committee should meet periodically with the independent auditor and the internal audit staff, if one exists, without the participation of management. Typically the auditors are asked whether there are any matters regarding the corporation and its financial affairs and records that make the auditors uncomfortable, whether the auditors have had any disagreement with management, whether the auditors have had full cooperation of management, whether the accounting systems and controls required are in place, and whether there are any material systems and controls that need strengthening.

F. Major Changes in Accounting Principles

Corporations have the power to choose the accounting principles and practices that are applied in the preparation of financial statements, subject to standards and limitations established by generally accepted accounting principles. The Audit Committee should review major issues regarding accounting principles and practices that could significantly affect a corporation's financial statements.

G. Legal Compliance and Codes of Conduct

A significant aspect of the board's responsibility, often referred to the Audit Committee, is oversight of the corporation's policies and procedures regarding compliance with the law and with significant corporate policies. Most large, publicly owned corporations have adopted codes of conduct expressing principles of business ethics, legal compliance, and other matters relating to business conduct. Subjects commonly addressed by such codes are legal compliance (antitrust laws and policies, Foreign Corrupt Practices Act of 1977, and insider trading, to name a few), conflicts of interest, corporate opportunities, gifts from business associates, misuse of confidential information, and political contributions. The board of directors should assure itself that the corporation has such a code of conduct, that the code is widely circulated to appropriate employees, that adherence to the code is enforced, that the corporation maintains procedures for monitoring and enforcing compliance, and that the support of the CEO and the board is clearly evidenced.

A program of legal compliance that is well conceived and properly implemented can significantly reduce the incidence of violations of laws and corporate policy. It may also reduce or eliminate penalties or prosecution against the organization for those violations of law that occur in spite of such a program. Since the enactment of the United States Sentencing Commission's Sentencing Guidelines for organizations, corporations have been given further reason to review and reassess their compliance policies and procedures. Although these guidelines greatly increase the penalties for businesses found guilty of criminal violations, they provide significant fine reductions for convicted corporations that maintain effective programs to prevent and detect violations of law.

H. Other Responsibilities

The Audit Committee may also be assigned other responsibilities, especially tasks related to the reliability of the corporation's financial results and related matters, such as preliminary review of annual and quarterly financial reports of the corporation, and review of periodic filings with the SEC.

SECTION 9

The Compensation Committee

The 1978 edition of the *Corporate Director's Guidebook* stated that the existence and function of the Compensation Committee have been largely overshadowed by the widespread attention given to the Audit Committee. Times have changed. Executive compensation has become *the* issue of discussion in today's corporate governance debate.

The executive compensation debate revolves around four questions:

- Are the CEO and the other senior executives paid too much?
- Is their compensation reasonably related to personal and corporate performance?
- Are their post-employment benefits properly related to the overall benefit of the corporation and reasonable in amount?
- Is there effective oversight of management's compensation?

The Compensation Committee is at the center of that debate. When functioning responsibly, it not only addresses the first three questions but also provides credibility and substance to the concept of independent and effective oversight.

33

A. Membership

The Compensation Committee should be composed solely of nonmanagement directors. Insider relationships and interlocking Compensation Committee membership (with CEO-directors sitting on each other's Compensation Committees) are strongly discouraged and trigger additional proxy statement disclosures. Further, the presence of a management director on a Compensation Committee may make the grant of a stock option subject to the profit recapture provisions of the securities laws. Under the 1993 tax legislation, the presence of an interested director may also prevent a tax deduction for executive compensation in excess of $1 million.

As with board membership generally, diverse backgrounds and experiences can be useful when serving on a Compensation Committee. If the board has among its members a senior executive of another publicly held corporation, he or she may well be an appropriate choice for membership on a Compensation Committee, but the committee should not be composed solely of highly paid executives.

The CEO will often wish to meet with the Compensation Committee, but the CEO should neither be on the Committee nor participate in all of its meetings. The same is true of the company's senior compensation or human resources executive. To provide both the reality and the appearance of independent oversight, it is necessary to have Committee meetings without members of management present, particularly when the compensation of the CEO and other senior executives is determined.

B. Principal Functions

The functions of the Compensation Committee are well summarized in the ALI's *Principles of Corporate Governance*.

The Compensation Committee should:

(1) Review and recommend to the board, or determine, the annual salary, bonus, stock options, and other benefits, direct and indirect, of the senior executives.

(2) Review new executive compensation programs; review on a periodic basis the operation of the corporation's executive

compensation programs to determine whether they are properly coordinated; establish and periodically review policies for the administration of executive compensation programs; and take steps to modify any executive compensation programs that yield payments and benefits that are not reasonably related to executive performance.

(3) Establish and periodically review policies in the area of management perquisites.

In fulfilling the first of these functions, which is fundamental to its responsibilities and is the role most traditionally assigned to it, the Compensation Committee should generally recognize that compensation can play an important role in attracting, retaining, and motivating the management talent that is crucial to any corporation's success. The committee must also be sensitive to the widespread concern that CEOs and other senior executives are often paid too much, especially when the corporations they lead are not performing well. The Compensation Committee must, therefore, provide oversight to ensure that the corporation's compensation program is competitive and that it is closely related to both personal and corporate performance.

In determining how corporate performance should be rewarded, the Compensation Committee generally should ensure that a significant portion of an executive's compensation is connected to the long-term interests of the shareholders. There should be an appropriate balance between short-term pay and long-term incentives. Developing the appropriate balance while focusing on long-term shareholder interests is an important responsibility of the Compensation Committee.

The structure and components of an executive compensation package vary among industries and among companies. Company size, industry characteristics, competitive factors, location, and corporate culture are all relevant factors. There is no single "right" answer.

The Committee should also review the benefits and perquisites provided to company executives. Important among these are benefits provided upon retirement or other termination of employment. There is significant concern that these benefits are often not sufficiently related to job performance.

The proper design of a compensation program is just the starting point. Application of the program requires at least annual performance evaluations of the senior executives, and the Committee should keep the full board informed of the results. Monitoring is required, and the Compensation Committee should modify existing programs to avoid payments and benefits that are not reasonably related to performance. This requires periodic review of the programs themselves as well as the actual payouts that result.

C. Compensation Committee Report

The SEC proxy rules require a report from the Compensation Committee describing the performance factors on which the Committee relied in determining the compensation of the CEO, as well as a discussion of the Committee's general policies with respect to executive compensation. Although this report is not considered a liability-creating document by the SEC, the members of the Compensation Committee should review a working draft with care well before it is in final form, particularly since the report is made over their individual names. The entire board must submit a report if the corporation does not have a Compensation Committee or another committee specifically performing its functions.

D. Staff Support

Whether the Compensation Committee should hire its own compensation specialists or rely upon company personnel or company-selected outside specialists is a controversial issue. Each Compensation Committee must decide that issue on its own, based primarily on its satisfaction (or lack of satisfaction) with the services provided by corporate employees or by specialists selected by the corporation. In most instances, the Compensation Committee does not have or need separate or independent staff. To help preserve the independence of any compensation specialists, whether they be within the corporation or outside, they should have direct access to the Compensation Committee without the presence of the CEO or other senior company officers.

It is important that the Committee receive the information it requests in an unbiased manner. That information should include comparisons with peer companies, analyzed by size, complexity, and other relevant factors. Committee members need to satisfy themselves that the data provided to them is not biased; for example, they should ensure that all peer companies are included. The Compensation Committee may wish to pay its executives more or less than the competition, but it should have adequate and unbiased data to determine the norms within the industry and other comparable businesses.

E. Other Responsibilities

Other responsibilities that may appropriately be taken on by the Compensation Committee are:

- planning for executive development and succession; in that capacity, some Compensation Committees take on a broader role, actually planning for management development and evaluation of key personnel;
- considering indemnification issues, although these are often handled by the Audit Committee;
- reviewing expense accounts of senior executives;
- reviewing "fringe" benefits, such as loans made or guaranteed by the corporation; and
- reviewing and recommending to the board, or determining, the compensation of directors.

SECTION 10

The Nominating Committee

In the last quarter-century, there has been a dramatic change in thinking in the business and legal communities regarding the need for and purposes of a Nominating Committee. For example, the 1979 Corporate Laws Committee report on Overview Committees noted that "only a minority of publicly-held corporations have as yet established a Nominating Committee." By 1990, The Business Roundtable was advocating that each corporation have a Nominating Committee, with membership limited to nonmanagement directors, undertaking an expanded role. Today, the vast majority of large publicly held corporations have Nominating Committees and, if they are not already composed solely of outside directors, shareholder activist organizations are pressing for that change.

A. Membership

The Nominating Committee should be composed of directors who are not officers or employees of the corporation. That does not mean there is no role for the CEO. The CEO, although not a member of the Nominating Committee, will nonetheless be expected to have a significant role in recommending candidates and recruiting them for the board. The Nominating Committee Chair should have prominent involvement in the recruiting process in order to reinforce the perception as well as the reality that the invitee's selection is being made by the Committee and the board, and not by the CEO.

B. Principal Functions

The two principal functions of most Nominating Committees are to recommend to the board:

- the slate of nominees of directors to be elected by the shareholders (and any directors to be elected by the board to fill vacancies); and
- the directors to be selected for membership on the various board committees.

The Committee may also be authorized to recommend that individual directors be designated as chairs of board committees, particularly committees that perform oversight functions, such as the Audit, Nominating, and Compensation Committees.

C. Criteria for Board Membership

The principal qualities of an effective corporate director include strength of character, an inquiring and independent mind, practical wisdom, and mature judgment. In addition to these attributes, the Nominating Committee will want to establish particular criteria for board membership. These may include individual qualifications such as technical skills, career specialization, or specific backgrounds. Some criteria will change with time—today a corporation might seek new directors who are business executives, or who have foreign expertise; next year, candidates who bring a particular scientific or technical experience to the board may be more appropriate. Many corporations have increased diversity in the boardroom through adding qualified women and minority directors.

Some publicly held corporations impose term limits on directors and many have a mandatory retirement age. Some companies expect a director to offer to resign if the director's principal occupation changes.

D. Selecting Directors

The basic responsibility of the Nominating Committee is to recommend to the board or to the shareholders nominees for election to the board. In many situations, this entails review by the Nominating Committee of the performance and contribution

of their fellow directors as well as the qualifications of any proposed new directors. This review is a key element of good corporate governance because the board is likely to adopt the
Committee's recommended choices. The majority of shareholders are likely to vote for the nominees selected by the board. In
the absence of malfeasance, it is not likely that a director will be
removed during his or her term of office.

In structuring a search for a new director, many corporations have constructed a "profile" of various attributes that the
board currently lacks entirely or, in the view of the board or a
committee, needs to strengthen. Focusing on the strengths and
weaknesses of the current directors has, in many situations,
proved helpful in directing the search toward candidates who
can make a more significant contribution to the corporation.

One of the criticisms often directed against corporate boards
is that initial election (often by the board to fill a vacancy) is
tantamount to being awarded tenure until retirement age. A
thoughtful review by the Nominating Committee of a director
coming to the end of his or her term before deciding whether to
recommend reelection is the most effective mechanism to address this criticism. The Nominating Committee should evaluate
each director in light of that individual's participation and contribution, also using any standards or criteria developed for
board membership. The committee may find it helpful to seek
the views of the other directors. Considering the delicacy of the
interpersonal relationships involved, such a review requires a
procedure for director review that the board recognizes as fair
and evenhanded.

E. Selecting Committee Members
The role of the Nominating Committee in some corporations
has been broadened to include making recommendations to the
board regarding the responsibilities, organization, and membership of board committees. The Nominating Committee may recommend to the full board the types and functions of board
committees, the qualifications for membership on each committee, the extent to which there should be a policy of periodic
rotation of directors among the committees, and any limitations

on the number of consecutive years a director should serve on any one board committee.

F. Management Directors

The CEO may recommend to the Nominating Committee that other senior officers of the company be appointed to the board. As noted in the ALI's *Principles of Corporate Governance*, "recommendations as to nominees made by the chief executive officer for directorships to be filled by other senior executives should normally carry very substantial weight." However, any such recommendations should also be considered in view of the size and structure of the board, given the current trend toward having fewer, and certainly less than a majority of, management directors on the board.

Senior officers who are also directors may be reluctant to take a position contrary to that espoused by the CEO. Accordingly, some argue that the attendance at board meetings of such senior officers in a nondirector, nonvoting capacity is sufficient to ensure that directors have ready access to all necessary information regarding the business and operations of the corporation, without compromising the independence of judgment that an effective director must enjoy. However, the nonmanagement directors may wish to utilize one or more board positions to evaluate the succession prospects of certain individuals and to ensure that they themselves develop a peer relationship and firsthand contact with senior executives who have detailed knowledge of the corporation's business.

G. Management Succession

The Nominating Committee is increasingly vested with the responsibility for recommending to the full board a successor to the CEO when a vacancy occurs through retirement or otherwise. The Nominating Committee often also reviews and approves proposed changes involving other senior management positions, with the understanding that the CEO is given considerable discretion in selecting and retaining members of the management team. In order to carry out these functions, Nominating Committee members should actively and directly review the performance of the CEO and members of senior management. The Nominating Committee may also wish to consider establishing emergency procedures for management succession in the event of unexpected death, disability, or departure of the CEO and to review management planning for the replacement of other members of the senior management team.

SECTION 11

Other Oversight
Responsibilities

Directors have various other oversight responsibilities.
These include the following:

A. Philanthropic Activities

A corporation may devote a reasonable amount of its resources to public welfare or charitable, scientific, or educational
purposes. It is appropriate that a program of charitable giving
have a philosophy, purpose, budget, and realistic management.

B. Political Activity

Corporate officers and employees frequently participate
actively in the governmental process by seeking to influence
legislative activities, shaping regulations, or encouraging or pre-
venting government action. The actions and political positions
taken are often highly visible and may affect the reputation of the
corporation.

C. Employee Safety and Health, Environmental
Protection, and Product Safety

Corporate policies and practices with respect to employee
safety and health, environmental protection, and product safety
not only are matters of legal compliance but may also reflect
concerns and values that go beyond obedience to law. Particularly for manufacturing firms, compliance with environmental

standards, whether government-mandated or self-imposed, will have an important financial impact and may pose special problems of adequate public disclosure.

D. Employees

Employee issues have become of much greater concern to boards of directors. These include:

- commitment of the corporation to equal opportunity and a workplace free of discrimination;
- attention to the needs of currently retired employees and future retirees, particularly the handling of their pension and health benefits;
- privacy concerns and corporate policies and procedures relating to maintenance and safeguarding of computer and other corporate records, and monitoring of telephone and other electronic communications to or from employees; and
- fiduciary duties of plan fiduciaries, directors, and others under the Employee Retirement Income Security Act of 1974 (ERISA).

E. Crisis Management

In recent years, many corporations have adopted and familiarized their boards with crisis management programs designed to organize the response to a corporate crisis. Board-level participation may provide objective review of management's plans for response, lend credibility to the response, and ensure that board representatives are kept suitably informed.

SECTION 12

Duties Under the Federal Securities Laws

Federal and state laws regulate the disclosure practices and securities transactions of corporations and their directors, officers, and employees. The federal laws relating to securities are administered by the SEC and affect many aspects of the day-to-day operations of publicly owned corporations. Violations of the federal securities laws can result in imposition of significant criminal and civil penalties, not only on the corporation but also on directors individually. Directors need to be particularly attentive to their own and the corporation's compliance with these laws.

A. Insider Trading

The federal securities laws prohibit corporate insiders, including directors, and the corporation itself, from purchasing or selling securities, either in the open market or in private transactions, when they possess undisclosed material information about the corporation. The corporation or insider in possession of such information must "disclose or abstain from trading."

The federal securities laws also prohibit insiders from giving tips—either by revealing nonpublic material information concerning the corporation to others who may use it in trading, or by giving others recommendations to buy or sell based upon such information. Information is material if there is a substantial likelihood that a reasonable investor would consider it important in deciding whether to buy, sell, or hold a security. Viewed from another perspective, information is material if it would likely affect the stock price in a predictable direction. If there is any doubt whether information is material, legal advisers should be consulted or the information should be treated as material. In many instances, the federal securities laws also prohibit the receiver of tips, the "tippee," from acting on that corporate information.

Violation of these insider trading laws triggers strict sanctions. The violator is liable for any profit made or loss avoided. In addition, a court can assess a penalty against the trader or tipper of treble damages—three times the profits made or losses avoided. Criminal sanctions are also available. The SEC also has the authority to award informants who report a violation up to 10 percent of the amount of the penalty recovered.

The corporation's management can be helpful in providing directors with guidance whether at any given time there is any nonpublic material information concerning the corporation. Many corporations have developed procedures requiring directors to contact corporate counsel, the chief financial officer, or the corporate secretary before trading, permitting each proposed transaction to be reviewed in the light of the current state of public information. Some corporations follow the practice suggested by the NYSE-listed *Company Manual* of restricting insider trading in the corporation's securities to window periods following dissemination of annual and quarterly financial results. The growing corporate practice is to require that all trades be approved in advance and to prohibit insiders and their affiliates from trading in the corporation's securities for the two- to three-week period before the quarterly release of financial statements rather than creating any "safe harbor" periods.

Directors, officers, and principal (at least 10 percent) shareholders also are prohibited from selling the company's shares short and must deliver shares against a sale within twenty days.

B. Short-Swing Profits
Directors of publicly owned corporations must report to the SEC all of their holdings of, and transactions in, the corporation's equity securities and must disgorge to the corporation any prof-

its realized from buying and selling such shares within any six-month period. When a person first becomes an "insider" (a director, officer, or more-than-10-percent shareholder), a report of beneficial ownership of the corporation's stock must be filed (Form 3). Thereafter, whenever there is a change in beneficial ownership, a monthly (Form 4) or annual (Form 5) report must be filed. These reports must be filed on a timely basis to avoid disclosure of any delinquency in the corporation's proxy statement and to avoid potential civil monetary fines. An insider is normally considered to be the owner of securities that are in the name of a spouse or child living at home, and may be the owner of securities held in a trust of which the insider is a trustee, settlor, or beneficiary.

Profit disgorgement is required if an insider purchases the corporation's securities within six months before or after selling the corporation's securities and vice versa (i.e., sales within six months before or after buying). Any "profit"—measured as the match between the highest-priced sales and the lowest-priced purchases—must be paid over to the corporation. The requirement is intentionally arbitrary and applies to all transactions within any six-month period whether or not the individual had inside information or, in fact, made a profit on an overall basis. This provision is enforced effectively by the private Bar.

Certain transactions, such as the grant and exercise of stock options and the acquisition of securities under employee benefit plans, may be exempt from the "purchase" and "sale" triggers of the short-swing profit rules if certain procedural requirements have been satisfied. Absent an exemption, the receipt of options, the acquisition of securities through benefit plans, and the acquisition of a "derivative security" related to the value of the corporation's common stock normally will be considered to be a purchase of the underlying security, and could give rise to liability. In addition, other indirect changes in ownership, such as reclassifications, intercorporate transactions, pledges, and mergers may, in certain circumstances, also be considered a transaction for purposes of the short-swing profit rules.

Retiring or otherwise departing directors may be subject to profit recovery on transactions occurring after they have ceased to be a director. Thus, if a director purchases shares of the corporation, resigns, and sells shares within six months after the purchase, liability may be imposed for short-swing profits even though he or she is no longer a director at the time of the sale. In short, unexpected liability may result from the application of the short-swing profit rules. This is a highly technical statute, and it is suggested that legal counsel be consulted before committing to a transaction.

C. Sales by Controlling Persons

The securities laws generally require registration with the SEC of securities held by controlling persons (which may include directors) before they may be sold to the public, unless an exemption is available. The most common exemption available is provided by SEC Rule 144. In general, Rule 144 permits the sale of limited amounts of securities without registration if certain conditions are satisfied. For example, if the securities to be sold were acquired in a transaction not involving a public offering from the issuer or an affiliate of the issuer, they must be held for two years to be eligible for sale pursuant to Rule 144.

D. Registration Statements

Directors have a special responsibility for the accuracy of a corporation's registration statements filed with the SEC in connection with any offering of the corporation's securities to the public. A director, whether or not he or she signs the registration statement, is liable for any material inaccuracy or omission in the registration statement, including information incorporated by reference from other filed documents, unless a defense is available.

The director's primary defense to liability is "due diligence." To establish that defense, the director must show that, after reasonable investigation, the director had reasonable grounds to believe, and did believe, that the registration statement did not contain any materially misleading statements or omissions. Actions required by the director to satisfy the due diligence standard will vary with the circumstances. Directors are in any event well advised to satisfy themselves that in preparing the registration statement the corporation follows procedures reasonably calculated to ensure its completeness. They also should personally review for accuracy all matters in the registration statement, particularly within their knowledge and competence.

E. SEC Reporting Requirements

Federal law requires publicly owned corporations to file periodic reports with the SEC, including an annual report on Form 10-K, quarterly reports on Form 10-Q, and reports on Form 8-K for certain material developments, and to provide annual reports to shareholders. These reports are required to include specified financial and other information.

As a general rule, directors are not expected to verify independently the accuracy of underlying facts contained in the periodic reports filed with the SEC. However, they should be alert for any material inaccuracies or omissions of information in such reports and should satisfy themselves that there are procedures in place reasonably designed to ensure the timeliness, accuracy, and completeness of corporate reports. Each corporation should formulate procedures appropriate to its circumstances.

The corporation's annual report on Form 10-K is the most detailed of the periodic reports filed with the SEC, whose rules require that it be signed by a majority of the corporation's directors. Directors should take particular care with respect to the accuracy and completeness of this report. The section of the Form 10-K entitled "Management's Discussion and Analysis" is particularly important and should be read thoroughly.

F. Proxy Statements

Directors should be particularly attentive to the procedures followed in preparing the corporation's proxy statements and should review them carefully before they are disseminated to corroborate that there are no material misstatements or omissions. A director, even an outside director who was not directly involved in the preparation of a proxy statement, may be at risk if he or she fails to exercise appropriate care in connection with the disclosures made in the proxy statement. In some circumstances, the standard of liability may be one of mere negligence.

G. Compliance Programs

Many corporations have established securities law compliance programs. These programs are designed to ensure that the corporation makes complete, accurate, and timely disclosure of material information, complies with the registration requirements, and satisfies other securities law obligations. Programs like these also help ensure that directors and other insiders comply with insider trading laws. A compliance program that is well designed and administered may itself go a considerable way toward satisfying a director's due diligence obligations under the securities laws.

SECTION 13

Liabilities and Indemnification

Directors may incur personal liability for certain breaches of either their duty of care or their duty of loyalty or for failure to meet the requirements of certain other applicable laws such as the federal securities laws. If a director breaches a duty to the corporation or violates the law, but still meets the prescribed statutory standards for indemnification discussed below, the corporation is empowered to indemnify the director against liability and expenses incurred.

A. State Law Liability

The Model Act provides that directors who act in good faith, with the care an ordinarily prudent person in a like position would exercise under similar circumstances, and in a manner they reasonably believe to be in the best interests of the corporation have met their duty of care to the corporation. Courts have not often sustained damage awards against directors for breach of this duty but have instead indicated that they will impose liability for breach of the duty of care only in cases of obvious or prolonged failure to participate diligently and to exercise oversight or supervision. However, recent decisions of the Delaware Supreme Court have re-emphasized the need for directors to take an active, rather than a passive, role in meeting their duty of care if liability is to be avoided.

In transactions in which a director has a personal interest, extra precautions must be taken to avoid improper self-dealing and to satisfy the applicable legal requirements. The Model Act and most state corporate codes prescribe procedures that may be followed to obtain approval, authorization, or ratification of interested director transactions. The scope of protection gained from following these statutory procedures varies from state to state.

In addition to liability for breach of fiduciary duties, directors can also be liable for unlawful dividends or other distributions. Which distributions are unlawful and give rise to director liability varies from state to state. Generally speaking, unlawful distributions are those causing, or made during, insolvency or those violating applicable laws or the corporation's articles of incorporation.

B. Federal Securities Law Liability

As discussed in the preceding section, directors can be personally liable under the federal securities laws, in some cases even where they act in good faith. In some circumstances, negligence will by itself be sufficient to establish liability.

C. Liability Under Other Laws

Directors also may be subject to personal liability under other state and federal statutes (such as environmental laws). Good faith and careful monitoring of management programs directed toward corporate legal compliance should provide substantial safeguards against personal liability.

D. Limitation of Liability

A majority of the state corporation laws and the Model Act permit the corporation to eliminate or limit the liability of directors to the corporation or its shareholders for money damages for breaches of certain duties, most frequently the duty of care. For instance, the Model Act permits an optional charter provision eliminating or limiting directors' personal liability for money damages, except liability for the receipt of a financial benefit to which the director is not entitled, the intentional infliction of harm on the corporation, an unlawful distribution, or an intentional violation of criminal law. Protection from liability generally applies only to monetary liabilities to the corporation and its shareholders and not to injunctive relief or to liabilities to third parties.

E. Indemnification

The Model Act and most state corporation statutes specify the circumstances in which the corporation is permitted or is required to indemnify its directors against reasonable expenses and liability incurred in connection with their service as directors of the corporation. The basic standard for indemnification in the Model Act is that the individual director has acted in good faith and with a reasonable belief that his or her conduct was in the best interests of the corporation. In the case of criminal proceedings, the director must also have had no reasonable cause to believe his or her conduct was unlawful. The Model Act provisions, which have been adopted in substance by numerous states, give corporations the power to indemnify directors in actions by third parties, including class actions, for expenses (including attorneys' fees), judgments, fines, and amounts paid in settlement of the actions. In derivative actions brought in the name of the corporation itself, indemnification is allowed for expenses (including attorneys' fees), but when a director has been found liable, indemnification is allowed only with court approval. A recent amendment to the Model Act provides that amounts paid in settlement of a derivative action may be indemnified if approved by a court.

The Model Act provides that indemnification for reasonable expenses (including court costs and legal fees) is mandatory if the director has been wholly successful in the defense of any action, on the merits or otherwise. Indemnification is not mandatory if the director is not totally successful. In the case of settlements or certain adverse court determinations in third-party actions, indemnification is permitted if authorized by the court or upon a determination by a majority of directors not involved in the action, by the shareholders, or by independent legal counsel that the director met the applicable standard of conduct.

Some corporations have charter or bylaw provisions mandating indemnification whenever it is legally permissible, and many corporations have entered into indemnification contracts with their directors to provide mandatory indemnification whenever the applicable statute permits it.

F. Advance for Expenses

The Model Act and most state corporation statutes permit corporations to advance funds to directors to pay or reimburse reasonable expenses incurred by them in defense of a matter before the final disposition of the proceedings and before final determination of their right to indemnification for those expenses. Directors generally must provide the corporation with an undertaking to repay any funds advanced by the corporation if it is ultimately determined that they are not entitled to indemnification. As a general rule, the advance for expenses is discretionary and made on a case-by-case basis upon authorization of the board of directors, unless mandatory advance of expenses is required by articles of incorporation, bylaws, contract, or applicable statute. Provisions mandating only indemnification may not be construed as also mandating advance of expenses before conclusion of the proceedings. Thus, any intent to make advance of expenses mandatory should be clearly expressed.

G. Insurance

Corporations may purchase directors' and officers' liability insurance under which the corporation is entitled to reimbursement of any payment of indemnity claims. Insurance also may protect the director from the corporation's failure to pay such indemnity and, in some cases, from claims against which the corporation is not permitted to indemnify. Certain areas of activity, such as environmental or antitrust matters, are often excluded from coverage. Conditions in existence at the time application for insurance is made also may be excepted. Directors' and officers' liability insurance provides uncertain coverage in the case of punitive damages, excludes criminal penalties and fines, and is not available in every case. The insurance coverage provided under particular policy wording requires detailed analysis.

As with every insurance policy, care must be taken in completing applications and questionnaires. The Model Act and the relevant statutes of most jurisdictions permit the corporation to bear the expense of such insurance.

CONCLUSION

Risking repetitiveness, but reaching for proper emphasis, we conclude with these basic points:

- A corporate director must exercise independent judgment for the overall benefit of the corporation.
- To meet the duty of care standard, a corporate director must be diligent and invest significant amounts of time and energy in monitoring management's conduct of the business and compliance with the corporation's operating and administrative procedures.
- A corporate director is entitled to rely on reports, opinions, information, and statements of the corporation's officers, legal counsel, accountants, employees, and committees of the board on which the director does not serve, when under the circumstances it is reasonable to do so.
- The duty of loyalty requires that a director not use her or his corporate position to enjoy a personal benefit, gain, or other advantage at the expense of the corporation.
- Conflicts of interest (including corporate opportunity situations and a director's transactions with the corporation) are not inherently improper and should not be regarded as an adverse reflection on the board or the interested director. It is the manner in which an interested director and the board deal with a conflict situation that determines the propriety of the transaction and the director's conduct.
- Corporate directors who act within the framework of conduct outlined in this Guidebook will be performing their directorial functions competently and reducing the risk of

being charged with deficient individual performance as a director.

- This Guidebook should not be viewed as a substitute for legal consultation and advice.

BIBLIOGRAPHY

For those interested in reading further, we include a partial list of recent periodical literature on some of the major topics covered in the Guidebook. We have omitted, by and large, all treatises, as well as articles published before 1980. The remaining list is not exhaustive.

I. The Business Judgment Rule

American Law Institute, *Principles of Corporate Governance: Analysis and Recommendations* (1994)

Arsht, "The Business Judgment Rule Revisited," 8 Hofstra L. Rev. 93 (1979)

Balotti & Hanks, "Rejudging the Business Judgment Rule," 48 Bus. Law. 1337 (1993)

Block, Dennis J., Barton, Nancy E. & Radin, Stephen A., *The Business Judgment Rule: Fiduciary Duties of Corporate Directors* (4th ed. 1993)

Block, Radin & Maimone, "Derivative Litigation: Current Law Versus The American Law Institute," 48 Bus. Law. 1443 (1993)

Block, Radin & Maimone, "Chancellor Allen, the Business Judgment Rule, and the Shareholders' Right to Decide," 17 Del. J. Corp. L. 785 (1992)

Coffee, "New Myths and Old Realities: The American Law Institute Faces the Derivative Action," 48 Bus. Law. 1407 (1993)

Committee on Corporate Laws, "Other Constituencies' Statutes: Potential for Confusion," 45 Bus. Law. 2253 (1990)

Dooley, "Two Models of Corporate Governance," 47 Bus. Law. 461 (1992)

Dooley & Veasey, "The Role of the Board in Derivative Litigation: Delaware Law and the Current ALI Proposals Compared," 44 Bus. Law. 503 (1989)

Easterbrook & Fischel, "Close Corporations and Agency Costs," 38 Stan. L. Rev. 271 (1986)

Eisenberg, "An Overview of the Principles of Corporate Governance," 48 Bus. Law. 1271 (1993)

Eisenberg, "The Structure of Corporation Law," 89 Colum. L. Rev. 1461 (1989)

Goldstein, "Revision of the Model Business Corporation Act," 63 Tex. L. Rev. 1471 (1985)

Hamilton, "Reflections of a Reporter," 63 Tex. L. Rev. 1455 (1985)

Manning, "The Business Judgment Rule and the Director's Duty of Attention: Time for Reality," 39 Bus. Law. 1477 (1984)

Orts, "Beyond Shareholders: Interpreting Corporate Constituency Statutes," 61 Geo. Wash. L. Rev. 14 (1992)

Smith, "An Underview of the Principles of Corporate Governance," 48 Bus. Law. 1297 (1993)

Sommer, "Whom Should the Corporation Serve? The Berle-Dodd Debate Revised Sixty Years Later," 16 Del. J. Corp. L. 33 (1991)

Veasey, "Duty of Loyalty: The Criticality of the Counselor's Role," 45 Bus. Law. 2065 (1990)

Veasey, "Focus on Selected Counseling Issues Involving the Business Judgment Rule and the Duty of Loyalty," Presented to the 29th Annual Corporate Counsel Institute (1990)

II. Fiduciary Duties of Corporate Directors

A. Duty of Care

Arsht & Hinsey, "Codified Standard—Safe Harbor But Charted Channel: A Response," 35 Bus. Law. ix (1980)

Burgman & Cox, "Corporate Directors, Corporate Realities and Deliberative Process: An Analysis of the *Trans Union* Case," 11 J. Corp. Law 311 (1986)

Chiappinelli, "Trans Union Unreconsidered," 15 J. Corp. L. 27 (1989)

Cohn, "Demise of the Director's Duty of Care: Judicial Avoidance of Standards and Sanctions Through the Business Judgment Rule," 62 Tex. L. Rev. 591 (1983)

Comment, "Limiting Corporate Directors' Liability: Delaware's Section 102(b)(7) and the Erosion of the Duty of Care," 136 U. Pa. L. Rev. 239 (1987)

Comment, "Statutory Limitations on Directors' Liability in Delaware: A New Look at Conflicts of Interest and the Business Judgment Rule," 24 Harv. J. on Leg. 527 (1987)

Committee on Corporate Laws, "Corporate Director's Guidebook," 33 Bus. Law. 1591 (1978)

Dent, "The Revolution in Corporate Governance, Monitoring the Board and the Director's Duty of Care," 61 Bost. Univ. L. Rev. 623 (1981)

Eisenberg, "The Duty of Care of Corporate Directors and Officers," U. Pitt. L. Rev., vol. 51, 1990, pp. 945-972

Fischel, "The Business Judgment Rule and the Trans Union Case," 40 Bus. Law. 1437 (1985)

Hansen, "The Duty of Care, the Business Judgment Rule, and the American Law Institute Corporate Governance Project," 48 Bus. Law. 1355 (1993)

Hawes & Sherrard, "Reliance on Advice of Counsel as a Defense in Corporate and Securities Cases," 62 Va. L. Rev. 1 (1976)

Herzel & Katz, "Smith v. Van Gorkom: The Business of Judging Business Judgment," 41 Bus. Law. 1187 (1986)

Hinsey, "Business Judgment and the American Law Institute's Corporate Governance Project: The Rule, the Doctrine, and the Reality," 52 Geo. Wash. L. Rev. 609 (1984)

Macey & Miller, "Trans Union Reconsidered," 98 Yale L.J. 127 (1988)

Manning, "Reflections and Practical Tips on Life in the Boardroom After Van Gorkom," 41 Bus. Law. 1 (1985)

Moskin, "Trans Union: A Nailed Board," 10 Del. J. Corp. L. 367 (1986)

Quillen, "Trans Union, Business Judgment, and Neutral Principles," 10 Del. J. Corp. L. 465 (1986)

Schwartz & Wiles, "Trans Union: Neither 'New' Law Nor 'Bad' Law," 10 Del. J. Corp. L. 429 (1986)

Simmons, "Informed Decisionmaking by Directors: The Director's Right to Rely Versus the Duty to Investigate," 55 Miss. L.J. 571 (1985)

Sorenson, "Discretion and its Limits—An Analytical Framework For Understanding and Applying the Duty of Care to Corporate Directors (and Others)," 50 Wash. U. L. Q. 553 (1988)

Veasey & Manning, "Codified Standard—Safe Harbor or Uncharted Reef? An Analysis of the Model Act Standard of Care Compared with Delaware Law," 35 Bus. Law. 919 (1980)

B. Duty of Loyalty

Begert, "The Corporate Opportunity Doctrine and Outside Business Interests," 56 U. Chi. L. Rev. 827 (1989)

Block, Maimone & Ross, "The Duty of Loyalty and the Evolution of the Scope of Judicial Review," 59 Brooklyn L. Rev. (1993)

Brudney & Clark, "A New Look at Corporate Opportunities," 94 Harv. L. Rev. 997 (1981)

Chew, "Competing Interests in the Corporate Opportunity Doctrine," 67 N.C.L. Rev. 435 (1989)

Committee on Corporate Laws, "Changes in the Model Business Corporation Act—Amendments Pertaining to Director's Conflicting Interest Transactions," 43 Bus. Law. 691 (1988)

Committee on Corporate Laws, "Guidelines for the Unaffiliated Director of the Controlled Corporation," 45 Bus. Law. 429 (1989)

Committee on Corporate Laws, "Guidelines on Going Private," 37 Bus. Law. 313 (1981)

Eisenberg, "Self-Interested Transactions in Corporate Law," J. Corp. L., 1988, pp. 997-1009

Grantham, "The Content of the Director's Duty of Loyalty," J. Bus. L., 1993, pp. 149-167

Johnston & Alexander, "The Effect of Disinterested Director Approval of Conflict Transactions Under the ALI Corporate Governance Project—A Practitioner's Perspective," 48 Bus. Law. 1393 (1993)

Marsh, "Are Directors Trustees? Conflict of Interest and Corporate Morality," 22 Bus. Law. 35 (1966)

Palmiter, "Reshaping the Corporate Fiduciary Model: A Director's Duty of Independence," 67 Tex. L. Rev. 1351 (1989)

Small, "Conflicts of Interest and the ALI Corporate Governance Project—A Reporter's Perspective," 48 Bus. Law. 1377 (1993)

Levmore, "Strategic Delays and Fiduciary Duties," 74 Va. L. Rev. 863 (1988)

III. Board Structure and Operations

Allen, "Defining the Role of Outside Directors in an Age of Global Competition," *Corporate Governance Today and Tomorrow* (1992)

Bacon, Jeremy, *Corporate Boards and Corporate Governance* (1993)

Business Roundtable, "Corporate Governance and American Competitiveness," 46 Bus. Law. 241 (1990)

Business Roundtable, "Statement of Position Concerning the Role of Corporate Directors," 33 Bus. Law. 2083 (1978)

Gilson & Kraakman, "Reinventing the Outside Director: An Agenda for Institutional Investors," 13 Stan L. Rev. 863 (1991)

Hanson, "The Long-Term Perspective: One Institutional Investor's Point of View," *Corporate Governance Today and Tomorrow* (1992)

Hanson, "Shareholder Value: Touchstone of Managerial Capitalism," 69 Harv. Bus. Rev. 141 (Nov./Dec. 1991)

Heard, "The Evolving Role of the Outside Director, Perspective of the Institutional Investor," *The Evolving Role of Outside Directors* (1993)

Henning, "Corporate Law After the Eighties: Reflections on the Relationship Between Management, Shareholders, and Stockholders," 36 St. Louis U.L.J. 519 (1992)

Hinsey, "The Committee System and the Role of Outside Directors," *The Evolving Role of Outside Directors* (1993)

Johnson, "Can the Board of Directors Make a Difference?" Presented at the Annual Corporate Governance Review of the National Association of Corporate Directors, Oct. 22, 1990

Koppes, "Acting Like a 'Real' Owner," *Corporate Governance Today and Tomorrow* (1992)

Korn/Ferry International, *Board of Directors Twentieth Annual Study* (1993)

Lang, "The Evolving Role of Outside Directors: Background and Issues," *The Evolving Role of Outside Directors* (1993)

Leech & Mundheim, "The Outside Director of the Publicly Held Corporation," 31 Bus. Law. 1799 (1976)

Lipton & Lorsch, "A Modest Proposal for Improved Corporate Governance," 48 Bus. Law. 59 (1992)

Lorsch, "Real Ownership Is Impossible," 69 Harv. Bus. Rev. 139 (Nov./Dec. 1991)

Mace, Myles L., *Directors: Myth and Reality* (2d ed. 1986)

Mauk, Edwin S. & Giardina, James A., *Organization & Compensation of Board of Directors* (1984)

McLaughlin, "The Evolving Role of the Outside Director: Perspective of the Outside Director," *The Evolving Role of Outside Directors* (1993)

Millstein, "The Evolution of the Certifying Board," 48 Bus. Law. 1485 (1993)

Millstein, "The Evolving Role of Institutional Investors in Corporate Governance," *Corporate Governance Today and Tomorrow* (1992)

Tobin, "Evolving Fiduciary Duties of Directors," *The Evolving Role of Outside Directors* (1993)

Working Group on Corporate Governance, "A New Compact for Owners and Directors," 69 Harv. Bus. Rev. 141 (July/Aug. 1991)

IV. Committees of the Board

A. General

Committee on Corporate Laws, "The Overview Committees of the Board of Directors," 34 Bus. Law. 1937 (1979)

Kolb, "The Delegation of Authority to Committees of the Board of Directors: Directors, Liabilities," 9 U. Balt. L. Rev. 1989 (1980)

B. Audit Committee

Conference Board, *New Directors in Internal Auditing* (Research Report No. 946, 1990)

Greene & Falk, "The Audit Committee—A Measured Contribution to Corporate Governance," 34 Bus. Law. 1229 (1979)

Mautz, Robert B. & Neumann, R., *Corporate Audit Committees: Policies and Practice* (3d ed. 1980)

Reinstein, Callaghan & Briotta, "Corporate Audit Committees: Reducing Directors' Legal Liabilities," 61 U. Det. J. Urb. L. 375 (1984)

C. Nominating Committee

Bacon, Jeremy, *Corporate Directorship Practices: The Nominating Committee and the Director Practices* (1975)

D. Compensation Committee

Foulkes, *Executive Compensation: A Strategic Guide for the 1990's* (1991)

Friedheim, "Measuring Executive Performance," Presented at Corporate Governance Conference, Jan. 13, 1992

National Association of Corporate Directors, Report of Blue Ribbon Commission on Executive Compensation: Guidelines for Corporate Directors (1993)

V. Other Oversight Responsibilities

Chatov, "What Corporate Ethics Statements Say," 22 Calif. Management Review 20 (1980)

Coffee, "Beyond the Shut-Eye Sentry: Toward a Theoretical View of Corporate Misconduct and an Effective Legal Response," 63 Va. L. Rev. 1099 (1977)

Committee on Corporate Laws, "The Public Policy Committee of the Board of Directors," 38 Bus. Law. 211 (1982)

Committee on Corporate Laws, "Guidelines for Directors: Planning for and Responding to Unsolicited Tender Offers," 41 Bus. Law. 209 (1985)

Engel, "An Approach to Corporate Social Responsibility," 32 Stan. L. Rev. 1 (1979)

VI. Duties Under Federal Securities Laws

Block, Radin & Carlinsky, "A Post-Polaroid Snapshot of the Duty to Correct Disclosure," 1991 Colum. Bus. L. Rev. 139

Longstreth, "Reliance on Advice of Counsel as a Defense to Securities Law Violations," 37 Bus. Law. 1185 (1982)

White, "Outside Directors Under the Federal Securities Laws: Fraudulent Actors or Innocent Victims?" 21 Sec. Reg. L. J. 297 (1993)

VII. Indemnification and Insurance of Corporate Officials

Balotti & Gentile, "Elimination or Limitation of Director Liability for Delaware Corporations," 12 Del. J. Corp. L. 5 (1987)

Hamilton, "Reliance and Liability Standards for Outside Directors," 24 Wake Forest L. Rev. 5 (1989)

Hanks, "Recent State Legislation on D & O Liability Limitation," 43 Bus. Law. 1207 (1988)

Johnston, "Corporate Indemnification and Liability Insurance for Directors and Officers," 33 Bus. Law. 1993 (1978)

Johnston, "D & O Insurance Crisis: How to Fund Indemnification Arrangements," *Insights: The Corporate & Securities Law Advisor*, Aug. 1987

Lazar, "Form and Structure of Defense and Settlement Clauses in Directors' and Officers' Policies," *Directors' and Officers' Liability Insurance and Self Insurance* (Practicing Law Institute 1986)

Note, "Protecting Corporate Directors and Officers: Insurance and Other Alternatives," 40 Vand. L. Rev. 775 (1987)

Sparks, Johnston & Conan, "Indemnification and Directors' and Officers' Liability Insurance: The Legal Framework under Delaware Law," *The Crisis in Directors' & Officers' Liability Insurance: Advising Corporations on Alternatives, Indemnification & the Business Judgment Rule* (1986)

Thompson & Hockenjos, "Misrepresentation in the Policy Application and Rescission Actions," *Directors' and Officers' Liability Insurance 1992* (Practicing Law Institute 1992)

Veasey, Finkelstein & Bigler, "Delaware Supports Directors with a Three-Legged Stool of Limited Liability, Indemnification, and Insurance," 42 Bus. Law. 399 (1987)

Also from the Section of Business Law:

Guidebook for Directors of Nonprofit Corporations

Written for a general audience, the *Guidebook* is filled with practical advice and legal guidance to assist directors of all types of nonprofit corporations in their duties and obligations. It covers the legal principles as they apply to nonprofit corporations and explains what is required by law, and equally important, what is good corporate practice. Topics include:

- How boards work: what they do, how they do it, and for whom
- How to determine the directors' key responsibilities and effectively allocate their time
- What responsibilities can *and should* be delegated to committees
- The special risks to directors and ways to protect themselves
- The key federal income tax issues, including special reporting requirements, obtaining tax-exempt status, and the risks to losing it

Numerous Checklists and Suggested Questions

At the end of each chapter, the *Guidebook* includes a checklist and suggested questions, which highlight the issues that should be reviewed by the corporation's chair; board of directors; chief executive; executive, nominating, and audit committees; and legal counsel.

Inexpensive, and Discounts Available

Every member of a nonprofit board of directors or trustees, legal counsel, and others involved with nonprofit corporations should have a copy of this indispensable guide. So to encourage its wide use, the *Guidebook* is being offered at $19.95 each, with substantial discounts—up to 50%—available for bulk copies. See the order form for details.

1993   8½ x 11   118 pages   paper

ORDER FORM

Please send me:

_____ copies of *Guidebook for Directors of Nonprofit Corporations* (5070264) @

- ☐ $19.95 each (1–4 copies)
- ☐ $14.95 each (5–25 copies)
- ☐ $12.95 each (26–100 copies)
- ☐ $ 9.95 each (100–1,000 copies)

$_____ Subtotal

$_____ Tax: (DC—6%, IL—8.75%, MD—5%)

$_____ Handling: Orders up to $24.99 add $3.95
$25.00–$49.99 add $4.95
$50.00 + add $5.95

$ _____ Total

Payment:

- ☐ Bill me
- ☐ Check enclosed payable to the American Bar Association
- ☐ VISA ☐ MasterCard

Acct # _____ Exp. Date _____

Signature _____

Name _____

Firm/Org _____

Address _____
(no P.O. Boxes please)
City/State/Zip _____

Phone number _____
(in case we have a question about your order)

MAIL TO: American Bar Association
Publication Orders
P.O. Box 10892
Chicago, IL 60611

OR PHONE: (312) 988-5522

OR FAX: (312) 988-5568 anytime

book